No New Teacher Left Behind

Donna Hupe, M.Ed.

PublishAmerica
Baltimore

First printing

At the specific preference of the author, PublishAmerica allowed this work to remain exactly as the author intended, verbatim, without editorial input.

ISBN: 1-4241-9762-7
PUBLISHED BY PUBLISHAMERICA, LLLP
www.publishamerica.com
Baltimore

Printed in the United States of America

So many people have motivated me throughout my teaching career.

My special thanks to:

*my students who taught me the "good things" about life

*my colleagues at Haine Elementary and Middle Schools who taught me our main purpose was always to help our students

*my college students and student teachers who taught me the importance of sharing what I know so that they might make good choices

*my husband who taught me I should stop and really listen to what others were saying rather than be defensive

*my daughter who taught me that students have good days and bad days...that parents and teachers need to accept that

*my close friends who read my manuscript and urged me to publish it

and…

*God…who has put me on the path which gives me opportunities to share my blessings so I might insure that

NO TEACHER WILL EVER BE LEFT BEHIND!

Table of Contents

No New Teacher
Left Behind

FOREWORD

Teaching…a career which is probably the most valuable in the world. Think about it…anyone who is involved in other careers had teachers who prepared them for the jobs they have chosen. I also believe that for every person…there is at least one teacher who touched his/her future.

My book, *No New Teacher Left Behind*, provides an honest look at the various challenges new teachers may face. It is a description of existing policies and rules that need their attention and an outlook regarding the positive changes in education that are occurring for students.

It is very important to me that new teachers preserve the spirit…the passion…which they have when they enter the schools for their first jobs. Focusing on what is good and how one can remain positive are the keys to insuring that the "flame within each new teacher never extinguishes".

Students deserve the very best when it comes to

education. They deserve teachers who are constantly striving to find answers...teachers whose mission is to help all students, regardless of attitude and/or ability...and...teachers who want to change the systems which have truly failed and have lost sight in what is needed to meet almost every student's needs. In other words...students need teachers who will insure that students are "never left behind".

As you read this book, remember that I write this based on my 31 years of teaching in a private school and public schools. There may be those who ask..."Where is the research?" My answer to that question is..."The research is my own and it is an honest reflection of what truly is happening, can happen, and will happen."

My wish for all new teachers...may the flame within you constantly burn...may the desire to be the best teacher your students ever had also grow...and...may you discover that the journey you will travel...linked with "teaching"...is one which can lead to endless accomplishments when it comes to students and yourselves.

It is a pleasure to share my observations and my words of encouragement with each of you. May my thoughts stimulate your thoughts and point you in a direction that can only lead to positive outcomes!

CHAPTER 1
That First Day When
You Are Called Teacher

I remember so well...my first teaching experience. I had received my letter in the mail informing me that I had been selected to teach Kindergarten. I was stepping in as a substitute teacher for one semester due to a maternity leave. As I read the letter, I realized that my dream had come true. I only had a few weeks to get ready for the biggest day in my life...my first day as teacher.

The night before that day...I did not sleep at all. I went to bed and lay in that bed thinking about the next day...my first day. The emotions were so mixed...happy about getting a job...worried about doing the job correctly...excited about meeting my students...worried about whether they would like me or not...anxious about being at school early...worried that the alarm would not go off in the morning. Thus, I did not sleep!

I wish I had a video tape of my first day as a teacher. It was January whenever I took over for the kindergarten teacher who was on maternity leave. Her kindergarten students were very used to their routines and schedule by that time. Whenever I had met with that teacher...she had told me that all would go very well with both the morning and afternoon groups of students.

All went so quickly on my first day that I was done with everything I had planned quite early. In fact, there was about one hour left until dismissal. Suddenly, I felt very insecure because the students were waiting for me to continue with activities...activities I really did not have organized nor ready.

And then, I realized that I had a creative mind. Before I knew it...the one hour that I needed to fill with activities went by very easily. In fact, the next time I looked at the clock...it was time for my students to be dismissed and go home. My first day as a full-fledged teacher ended successfully. They actually wanted me to return the following day (some were saying they would see me tomorrow as they left).

Ah...the first time I called them "my students"...a memory, which you carry for a long time. And when you are shown your classroom, once you are hired...you just stand there looking at it calling it your "home away from home". You soon realize that it had become a reality...after years of undergraduate work in college...after many professors and classes...after what seemed about

100 papers and reports which demanded late night "staying awake until the last sentence was typed" and an eternity of preparation...you were finally someone who was called *teacher*...

Yes...it was a great feeling...one that lasted for many, many days...months...years...for me. It lasted for 31 years of my life. I never felt I lost the "feeling"...the passion for making a difference with students. However, there were various attempts to extinguish the feeling...to bring on other feelings that could overshadow the passion that was positive...to make the "feeling" non-existent.

And now...I find it is time to write a book that will protect the "positive feelings" that you, as a new teacher, have right now. That enthusiasm...that desire to be the best teacher in the eyes of your students and parents...that inventive feeling that motivates you to make everything you present interesting, never boring...those are the "feelings" I want to see burn within you so that you may develop a passion that can only bring about incredible learning.

As you read this book, keep in mind that I write this from the heart...a teacher's heart. The research that went into the chapters is really based on personal experiences...real-life experiences in various classrooms throughout the years.

My goal...to insure that new teachers will be the next generation of educators who do make the difference...who carry on what has been already established as successful practices…who eliminate practices that truly do not meet the needs of students…who see their extra efforts as a pay off for their students and themselves.

I want to make sure that "no new teacher is left behind"…

"Develop a passion that lights a fire within you…one that may flicker, but will never die…"

CHAPTER 2
Products on an Assembly Line
or Students

You are probably saying..."Wait a minute, you mean...no child left behind." On the contrary...that supposedly is being addressed by the government...our politicians...the administrators...the school boards...parents...community members...and...teachers...

I propose that we need to focus on what new teachers need in order to reach the goals linked with that popular phrase. I am not going to address higher salaries and benefits. No...I don't want to allow anyone reading this book the opportunity to lose focus by going down the list of reasons regarding why teachers don't deserve more money...reasons that point out "teachers only work nine months a year"...reasons that may bring out the people who tend to destroy the passion I mentioned I want to preserve in each of you.

Rather...I want you to focus on how to create the passion for teaching so that you can become the best you can possibly be. So...let's get started with the first concern I have and how you can stay focused so that the fire has a chance to start burning.

There were many times, during my last five years of teaching, I would sit back, after a week, and begin to wonder...where do I find the person who is responsible for making my job suddenly 70% paperwork and record keeping versus 30% teaching children? I felt as though I needed to eliminate some of the creative lessons...that I needed to make time for drills and more student paper pencil work...that I needed to change my belief system to a goal of increasing student test scores as opposed to increasing student thinking.

Well guess what...for 31 years, my classroom still generated an environment that provided time for creative thinking...time for talking about what was on my students' minds...and time for completing academic work that needed to be finished within a given year. I accepted that changes were occurring within education (well, I complained about them first...then had to accept them) and that district policy was something I had to follow if I was going to keep my job.

But...I also accepted the fact that in order for me to continue my job as a teacher...I had to meet my own needs...to create a classroom environment which invited students to come in and learn...to provide activities which promoted student success...to insure that my students had a place within a school which generated laughter and fun every day.

The key to living up to those expectations is being prepared for what is requested of you each school year. You will discover very soon that it is possible that curriculum may need to be revised year after year...that lesson plans may grow longer in size so as to follow federal and state mandates/anchors...that the test scores from the previous year of students just were not high enough and that you will be expected to "fix that problem" during the new school year.

And this brings me to my word of caution...watch out for schools that have come to believe they are businesses.

I remember going to a professional development presentation in which the speaker said, "teachers need to look at the students as products." I thought to myself..."Did I hear that person correctly? I believe he said that students need to be treated as if they are on an assembly line and we need to insure that each of them works properly...in other words, that they learn as much as possible so that test scores will reflect a school district that promotes student achievement."

You should know that I immediately went to the restroom for a moment to compose myself...

My first piece of advice to you...never, ever refer to students as "products". Rather, remember that they are people. Students are the "young people" we are to be focused on, at all times...who come first, no matter what the situation. They are the "people" who look to us for guidance...for leadership...for advice...for help. They are the "people" who need to know that teachers really care and do not look at them as robotic devices whose main goal is to generate test scores that are above certain percentages.

You will discover very quickly that school systems are striving to operate as educational businesses. There is even a possibility you were taught that in your undergraduate studies. The primary reason is because of "No Child Left Behind" which has placed a major emphasis on student achievement and teacher account-ability. Both of those are very significant. I support the ideas of helping students improve and accomplish as much as possible within the schools, and I agree with teachers being held accountable so that those things can occur.

The thing I would remind you about as a new teacher...stay away from getting caught up in treating your students as if they were "products on an assembly line". Trust me...that type of attitude can occur whenever a school district continuously stresses that student test scores measure how well a teacher has taught during a given year. There are tales of some school districts making an attempt to tie test score results with teacher evaluations.

But how, Donna, can I stay away from having a business mentality if the district in which I teach motivates that type of thinking? Good question.

My best advice to you...remember that you are a teacher...not a manager...not a business executive...not a CEO. Your job is to insure that your students reach the expectations you set. If you stay on course with that mindset...then your students will be successful and will live up to what the school district wants to see from you.

Whenever we stray from that course...and begin to look at the student test scores as the only means to our being looked at as successful and our being "validated" as an exceptional teacher...then we will discover that our students do not choose to learn...do not have the desire to do their best...and certainly will not remain interested in what we are teaching them each day. The outcome...I'm sure you can predict it for yourself.

I do understand the nation's concern when it comes to education in the United States. I also understand why politicians decided to create policies that focused attention on student assessment, teacher accountability, and school achievement. The thing I do not accept is that in order to reach those goals a teacher must sacrifice key components in lessons which bring about student interest and promote motivation. These components would be creative thinking, time for class discussions, teachable moments, and the old fashion "let's bag the lesson...it's snowing" kind of mentality.

Stay convicted to the belief system that you, as the teacher, can help your students improve their test scores by providing lessons, which stimulate their thinking. The phrase "drill and kill" is one to truly think about...for if we do go back to the old school mindset of "the only way students will master a skill is by paper/pencil tasks" we surely will then produce the robot like products that professional development presenter, I mentioned earlier, had in mind.

May you, the new teacher, join the group of educators who remain dedicated to the thought that teachers and students can enjoy what they do together...and can experience the learning that truly matters in a lifetime.

"Students deserve being treated as young people who have social, emotional, and academic needs...teachers deserve being allowed to meet those needs every day."

CHAPTER 3
Did You Tell Them Who You Are?

I think back to the times whenever I would go out into the community in which my school district was located...to shop at the local grocery store or go to a restaurant with my husband and daughter. And yes...I was one of those women who had to make sure I had make-up on my face and was dressed in a casual way. Well...you never knew what parent and/or student you may see whenever you were out doing errands. I wanted to make sure that "Mrs. Hupe" looked presentable at all times...what a crazy thought.

However...I must tell you...image is a very significant part of being a teacher. I support the thought that teachers are true role models and that they should live up to the expectations that may be linked with that description. Students do look to you when it comes to answers...whenever it comes to knowing right from wrong...in situations which may lead them to form opinions about this world in which they are living. I cannot think of a time, during those 31 years of teaching, I ever strayed from the mindset that I needed to practice good values and that I needed to follow God's plan, that being a personal choice that plays a significant role in my life.

You need to let your students know who you really are. That does not mean...that if you have some political or religious agenda...that you should use the classroom as your stage for preaching. Rather, I mean that students can benefit whenever they realize that teachers are real people...with families, with pets, with hobbies, and with many diversified interests outside of the classroom.

I was always surprised that students did not really believe that I had a life beyond teaching. Seriously...whenever I would do my "suitcase act" (will explain that in a moment)...they would look at me as if they were discovering something brand new about Mrs. Hupe...something that they could not conceive as truth. I always felt, though...that sharing "myself" with my students was quite important. I believe it allowed them opportunities to relate better with me and I experienced, many times, that students believed my advice because I had shared some personal experiences with them which were similar to those they were living.

Let me give you an example. Whenever I went to school...I was classified as a "nerd". I actually would bring in pictures of what I looked like whenever I was in elementary school and junior high school. They depict a girl who was very tall...with big feet (I think I have worn a size 10 shoe since second grade)...who always had to wear glasses. My hair was sometimes short...sometimes curly (I had an aunt who wanted to be a beautician and, because she never became one, she practiced on me). I was that person who would overhear others being invited to parties...who listened to conversations about boyfriends...who earned great grades in school but never high grades from her peers that deemed her a part of the "popular crowd".

I always shared that with my students...as young as those in Grade 2. The best opportunity was whenever I taught middle school (Grades 5 and 6). I would have to say those are the years whenever students are in a time warp...whenever their bodies are changing and they are trying to figure out do they go backwards, where it is safe as an elementary student or move forward, where it is time to be a pre-teenager. I discovered that whenever I brought in my pictures and told a few stories about how I felt as that "person" of long ago...it seemed to establish a relationship with my students.

One time...I actually had a second grade student say, "I feel sorry for you, Mrs. Hupe". Wow...that was pretty powerful...I had not meant for my students to feel sorry for me...rather, I wanted them to realize that I had evolved from that time into a fine woman...a person who now wore contacts...who had a great problem solving mind...and who had accepted whom she was.

The point in all of this...tell your students about yourself. Do it the first day of school. I mentioned the "suitcase act". I found a vintage suitcase near Pittsburgh...in one of those great shops on the Southside. Each year...I would load up that suitcase with my "artifacts"...pictures of me whenever I was young, pictures of my family and dog, items which represented my many interests. I would pull out each item and tell my students about how that item tied in with me. It took about 20 minutes.

Then I would set up a display so that students could come up and examine the "artifacts"...kind of like the Mrs. Hupe Museum.

The next step...to find out about my students. Each student would take the suitcase home and bring it back with his/her own personal items...to tell the story about them. I included a sheet that explained to parents what I had done and what I was doing. The "suitcase act" has to be one of the best memories I will ever cherish.

This suggestion is to be used with every age of student...so secondary teachers, do not think for one moment that your high school students would not enjoy knowing about you and your many interests. Of course...there will be those students who display an attitude of "Who cares about you?" However, in the end...you will discover that even those students are tuned in to what you are telling them.

Remember...you are making every attempt during the first week to establish who you are and what you will expect. It is a matter of convincing your students you are sincere about what you say...that you are a person who has experienced life in many different ways and has become a teacher who wants to share those moments to prepare students for what may lie ahead.

**Tell your students about who you really are...
how you got to where you are
at that given moment in time!**

CHAPTER 4
Help! I've Got Paperwork and I Can't Get Done!!!

And now...for a chapter that reveals a little more about me (I'll be sure to live up to what I just told you in the previous chapter). You need to know whom Donna Hupe really is...sometimes a complainer and usually a person who will make changes when someone gives her a thought to consider.

I remember the day when my district informed us that we would be completing lesson plans that were more detailed. The key word...detailed (beware of when someone tells you that you need to improve what you write by adding details when it comes to lesson plan objectives, procedures, and assessments). The training for this lasted a few minutes...at least that is what it felt like. Instead of plans which actually depicted what was to be completed each day...I was supposed to write plans that "itemized" every happening…every minute…every goal that each student had to reach on a daily basis (sometimes I felt like it was a "total minutes" basis…).

Suddenly…I was doing more work than I had ever done before. The time it took me to write out one daily lesson plan was equal to about 45 extra minutes. That is not an exaggeration. The total pages of the weekly lesson plans were usually about 10 to 12 pages…this being a change in comparison to one sheet typed per day.

I believe I was complaining in the copy room…regarding this new event in my teaching life. The complaining was always easy because most of the other teachers felt the same way. The list of "why this was really crazy" had grown to equal what our weekly plans actually included in lengths of pages. However…on one particular day…there was a good friend…a veteran teacher…who actually said that these plans were motivating her to focus more and to really stay on task when it came to teaching each day plus reaching the weekly goals of the units we were teaching. She felt more organized.

I think it was the way she said it…it was as if she was confessing something and, at the same time, revealing that she had been saved! Yes…that's a good way to describe the moment. And what was I doing??? I was standing there…with my mouth closed…listening to that inner voice we all have that was saying, "You know she is right…"

Here's the point when it comes to the paperwork…we

have to accept that this is part of the job. That does not mean we cannot continue striving to work with our administrators, who in many cases do understand and would like to provide more time for each of us, to change requirements and insure that the plans are useful tools rather than hindrances. There are great templates which offer organized plans and which do identify student objectives, your teacher procedures and materials, and which identify the tools for assessing whether the students mastered the skill(s).

As a new teacher, you will need to find out what is expected of you each week when it comes to completing lesson plans and following district policies. Once you have been informed, and hopefully trained on this matter, then you can begin organizing your seven days per week so that there is time for completing the required paperwork.

My best advice...pick one day/one evening when you know you can complete the following week of plans. Too many times...teachers are distracted and/or interrupted when attempting to complete the written tasks demanded of them in school. Just as our students are taught to set aside a study time and to set up a good study environment at home...this too should be your rules when it comes to getting your schoolwork completed.

Many times...school principals will request that lesson plans and other important activity sheets be handed in to them by a certain day of the week. Hopefully, that is Monday. Use one of the weekend days (they have become a part of the number of days we work during the school year). It is a matter of deciding which of the two days you will use to complete this work.

If the plans are due on Friday...then you might consider my second piece of advice...work on Tuesday, Wednesday, and Thursday...splitting up the paperwork and working within set time limits.

It is a matter of examining your days and the times when you still have the energy to complete this type of work. Trust me...the first year will be the most challenging. The second year will bring with it a sense of familiarity when it comes to the curriculum, the resources you will be using, and the lessons/units you will be teaching.

Let me also insert in this chapter... checking student work...

One option is to use the weekend to check student work. You can then set up a policy with your students that allows them to hand in their weekly work by Friday. The key...you must correct the work and hand back to your students on Monday. Once you establish this type of routine...you will find that you then have time during the week to possibly complete the lesson plans and prepare the necessary materials/activity sheets that will be used during those daily lessons.

One of my past student teachers, presently a veteran

teacher of 14 years, reminded me that this option might lead to burn out for some individuals. So the other option is to either use time you may have, called "prep or planning time" within school (this demands discipline on your part...staying in your classroom with the door shut usually will work so you have the 30 or 40 minutes uninterrupted) or to check the papers immediately after they are handed in by your students that day. This can be achieved sometimes by using time before and/or after school. Instead of talking with colleagues in the morning over coffee...set up a routine that on Tuesday, Wednesday, and Thursday mornings/late afternoons you will check student papers so as to not take any home over the weekend. Then Saturday or Sunday is strictly devoted to completing the lesson plans and other required paperwork.

As that veteran teacher had implied...lesson plans can be used as an important tool which keeps you focused on what you are to be doing each day and each week. Requirements differ from school to school...district to district...and state to state. No matter what these may be...it is a matter of following a consistent routine when it comes to getting your work completed. Like I said earlier...think of yourself as a student who is making an attempt to complete assignments on time and as accurately as possible.

I discovered quickly...my plans and other work were completed more easily when I closed my mouth and accepted that I just had to do the work. I also continued to work with my peers and the administrators to find better...more efficient ways...of reporting what needed taught each week. It is very certain that there are districts, somewhere in the United States, which have supported their teachers' efforts and truly see their time as very valuable. Those are the districts we should be using as models when it comes to completing the clerical responsibilities.

"Establish a routine...create a work environment that is conducive to completing the teacher work you must finish each week."

CHAPTER 5
Making the Student Connection

One of the most asked questions from student teachers seems to be "How do I build a rapport with my students?" Whenever student teachers are assigned to classrooms during that final year in college, many seem to marvel at how their cooperating teachers build that connection with the students. This is especially true for student teachers who have walked into a second semester situation. By January, the best teachers have developed relationships with their students that are wonderful to watch in action. The relationships can range from incredible respect and trust on the parts of elementary students and their teachers to a friendly "give and take" between teachers and their secondary students.

So...how do you establish that connection? My strong advice on this one...stay away from creating a relationship that suggests you want to be your students' best friend.

That is not what your identity is in the classroom. Rather, you are to be the leader...the advisor...the person with the knowledge who can bring about learning experiences for the students that will be applicable and memorable.

Please be sure you read that correctly. I said... "stay away from creating a relationship that suggests you want to be your students' best friend". I did not say... "do not have a friendly rapport with your students". Both statements are clearly different.

Sometimes the newest and youngest teachers work to establish a friendship with their students during their first year of teaching. The reason is primarily because newly hired teachers (as well as all teachers) want to be liked by their students. These teachers in establishing a friendship...begin to see classroom management sacrificed.

You see...when you are friends with your students...just as when you are pals with your "personal friends", you tend to overlook certain behaviors that you know are unacceptable or not positive. Again...the reason that can happen in situations where teachers are striving to establish a friendship is because they want to insure that the students will like them every day of the school year.

The classroom that offers a "friendly environment" will be the more successful one when it comes to student respect and teacher rapport with the students. You will discover that students will feel comfortable...and that is truly what you want to establish in your classroom...a comfort level that establishes a feeling of "I feel safe...I feel respected by my teacher...I matter as a student."

How do you create that type of environment? Well...one thing is for sure...smile in front of your students. There is a tale (I never knew if this was a truth or not) that some professors in college have instructed their education majors to "not smile until November or December." Possibly...you have heard that before. Please...do not follow that instruction. Smiling is probably the one ingredient that sends the message to your students that you are a friendly teacher. I cannot imagine a teacher who frowns or holds the mouth firm every day depicting that teacher who motivates the students to buy into what is being taught.

The other thing you can do is make sure your students understand what you deem as the policies within your classroom. I always presented a lesson, on the first day of school, which offered the students a chance to decide what rules/procedures needed to be in place so that learning could occur. Trust me...students as young as second graders can tell you what behaviors are acceptable and which behaviors are unacceptable. Once you establish the list...consider having them displayed in the classroom...possibly even signed by the students.

I also suggest you ask your students what "behaviors" they would like to see you exhibit as the teacher. Again...students can offer some very good ideas with regards to how they would like their teacher to act each day. Of course, I discovered that the number one behavior students did not ever want to see was the teacher yelling at a student or the students. This was always...always...their first concern.

As new teachers...go back to when you were in school and write down the names of teachers you may have had who provided classrooms and learning environments that felt "friendly" to you. Then write down a list of things they each did that enabled those things to occur. You had great mentors...teachers who were your favorites...and, in most cases, I am willing to bet they were teachers who could be strict and could be quite compassionate...all on the same day or during the same class period.

You will make great connections with students throughout your lifetime of teaching. Be sure to start on the right foot by providing an environment that gives your students a fair chance when it comes to enjoying the learning you wish them to acquire.

"Provide a classroom that offers a friendly atmosphere...stay away from establishing personal friendships with your students."

CHAPTER 6
Parents...Here They Come!

Now for the topic about which new teachers are usually most concerned...the topic related to parents. There are many things I could share about parents based on 31 years of teaching. However, I am going to focus on the things I believe cause new teachers to be anxious.

First...remember...the majority of parents are very supportive and positive when it comes to teachers and their children's education. So many times, we hear the phrase..."It's the parents' fault." In a few cases...that particular statement is quite true. In many cases, the statement is false.

You need to remember that parents are facing a great deal of obstacles and challenges in this world we call home. Whenever I think about my 31 years of teaching and the span of time when the most changes occurred in education, I focus on the last ten years. The reason...because it is during those years that so many things occurred...9/11, invasion into Iraq, the threat of terrorists, challenges to the safety in the schools, the "easy" availability to drugs and alcohol...the list is endless. The things that happened throughout those years have truly made "being a parent" a constant challenge...especially when it comes to knowing the needs of your child and meeting the needs so that your child will be successful and safe.

I want to also make sure that you know another truth about me...I was a teacher who sometimes participated in criticizing "parents" and blamed them for the students' lack of interest in school. Were there times when that accusation was true...yes. However, whenever I look back and think about the different instances...the problems were a combination of things. I believe that there were times when I did not want to believe that I was a contributor. Why, I was a great teacher...how could it ever have anything to do with me?

I suggest that whenever you are dealing with some type of student problem...look at the problem from the perspective "How can the parents and I work together to help this student?" In every instance, whenever I strived to communicate with the parents...together we were able to find some solution. You should also accept that there will be solutions that work the first time and there will be other times when there needs to be a Plan B, Plan C, and so on.

Parents really are people who care about the children and teenagers they love. In the majority of the cases, you will find that they can be just as nervous about meeting you, the teacher, as you are about meeting them.

One of the best things schools can offer is a "parent night". This is not an Open House. Rather, this is an evening when parents come to listen to you and to learn about your plans for the school year. That meeting, when organized well, can be one of the most beneficial events at the beginning of the school year that you could provide. Be sure to tell them about who you are (ah...remember that chapter?), what your expectations regarding behavior and homework policies will be, and why you guarantee that the school year will be a great one for their children.

Yes...you will be nervous. I would rather see you provide a meeting like this than not communicate one thing with the people who "want to know" as much as they can at the beginning of the school year.

In the event, you have a parent(s) who chooses to come in to such a meeting and "badger" you...make sure you have discussed with your colleagues, whose classrooms are near yours, and/or your principal about what suggestions they may have for you regarding this type of situation. My advice...tell that parent you will talk with him/her during a personal conference which can be scheduled after the meeting. In most cases...that will work.

What if you cannot hold a meeting in the evening? Then you need to create a newsletter that is either sent by you personally in the mail (pay the postage…it will be well spent) or is given to the students to take home. I prefer you mailing the newsletter. That way you know that the parents probably received your correspondence. Again…outline who you are, what your expectations will be, and how you plan to insure that the students are in a classroom that promotes learning. I suggest no more than two pages, front and back.

You will be expected to participate in parent conferences. The number of scheduled conferences per year depends on the school district's policies and/or the needs of the student. This is another occurrence that can bring on anxiety and no sleep for new teachers the night before. The best thing you can do is talk with another colleague and/ or your principal to learn about various suggestions on how to hold the conferences. I am sure you will find someone who is willing to help you, especially in planning your very first meetings. If not…e-mail me with your specific questions and I will help you plan so that you have every opportunity to feel successful as the leader of the conferences (e-mail address will follow at the end of this book).

There will be parents who are very positive…who support your efforts in every way. There will be others who may question decisions you make…but who still display a respect towards you and who are thankful you would discuss their inquiry. And…there will be a few…and I stress a few…who have agendas that are beyond what you, as a teacher, are capable of following. In the case of the latter...rely on that mentor and/ or those administrators to help you get through the school year and remain professional. These types of parents who, for whatever reason, believe they have certain rights to be disrespectful, accusatory, and just plain nasty, probably lead (sad) lives which very rarely bring them anything positive.

Your focus is always to be on your students. In every event...regardless of the type of parent(s) who is linked with a student...you, the teacher, owe the student the attention he/she deserves in order to be successful in school. Hopefully, you will experience what I did...supportive parents who truly wanted to work with me instead of against me.

I am very confident that you, as the new teacher, will do just fine. The main reason will be...you want to make a positive difference in each student's life...and, in order to make that happen, you will want to create opportunities for connecting you at school with the parents at home.

"Parents are not our enemies, as we may think or be told...rather, they are people who are looking for successful schools who promote learning and a safe environment for their children. Strive to find the ways to work with them...not against them."

CHAPTER 7
Keeping Secrets

This chapter is probably, for me, one of the most important I will write for you as a new teacher. I want to encourage you to follow an important rule whenever you are teaching. You will find that if you do remember what I am about to tell you...you will, I believe, be a teacher who can be trusted by many.

The rule...remember that information about students should always be confidential. That is also true of parents and other colleagues you may work with in the school. However, I want to devote this chapter mostly to students because I believe that we, as educators, sometimes forget this rule and find ourselves talking about students in ways that truly are not helpful.

You may be saying to yourself, "What is so important about that rule? Why would you consider this chapter to be one of the most important? Of course I will keep information confidential." Well…that is easier said than done.

Sometimes whenever you learn about a student's personal background or you may learn about that student's home environment as being non-supportive…you will find you want to share that information with another. It may be a colleague at school or it may be your spouse or roommate…whatever the case…there can be a need within you that strongly motivates you to tell the "secret" to someone else.

The reasons are varied. If the student is one who causes you a great deal of stress because you cannot reach him/her…then you may want to share the information because you want to have someone support you by saying, "That is quite a terrible situation…" or maybe you want someone to agree with you that what you are enduring just is not fair.

There can also be times you may be tempted to sit with a group of your colleagues and begin to "let out" everything about a student. Again…you are feeling the need to "vent"…to have your colleagues rally around you and tell you that it is the student's fault as opposed to yours.

It happens…pure and simple. What is the key to insuring that whatever you say does not end up at the supermarket as a point of discussion among parents…or does not end up getting back to a student…or does not end up being learned about by the parent? The key is to think about what you are saying and where you are saying it.

You see…I am not telling you, especially as a new teacher, that you will not be able to talk with another professional about how to help a student who may be struggling or one who may not be behaving acceptably in your classroom. You will have avenues within the school which provide the right opportunities to discuss a student's performance and progress. There are various policies in place within the schools that allow for a means to seek information about how you, as the teacher, can incorporate the correct procedures so that the student has the chance to improve.

You must realize that whenever it comes to discussing a student…a teacher must always remember that the focus is to be on "How can I help this student?" In some cases, you can possibly talk to another colleague about a student…but I would impress upon you that it may be better to discuss that student by not using a name. If you are truly seeking out the means for changing something in your classroom so as to benefit that student…then you can share the situation you are enduring with another peer by not being specific as to whom the child is.

You can also talk with your principal about a student. Administrators are bound to confidentiality…just as guidance counselors, support team teachers and staff, nurses, and personnel who may be involved with students who have special needs.

It is staying away from the temptation to talk about a student when you are out at a restaurant or whenever you might be in the community…those are the times you must remind yourself that each student has the right to confidentiality. The only place you should be discussing information about a student is in the school.

This area is one that is becoming an increasing challenge for teachers. There is sometimes no place for a teacher, who may be struggling due to challenging student, to go when that teacher needs support. I praise those school districts that have created the "support team" approach which allows for teachers to attend meetings with documentation so that they can professionally discuss options for handling situations they may be facing with a student. These districts are focused on the student and provide for teachers a forum which will include other experts who can contribute ideas and suggest what may work better.

May you always, as a new teacher, know what outlets are available to you when it comes to needs you will experience with students and parents. Be sure to know what plans, at your school, are in place to help you whenever you are having trouble with a student. You will find that when you use those avenues...confidentiality will stay in place and the outcome will be a good one for you and your students.

"Respect your students when it comes to personal information."

CHAPTER 8
Getting Along with Others

I find it interesting that I would have this chapter in this particular book for new teachers. However, just as previous chapters have been based on 31 years of experience in the world of education...so will this particular chapter that deals with building relationships with your colleagues in the school and within the school district.

There are districts that take into consideration that new teachers will exhibit many needs during their first year of teaching. Whenever they do acknowledge that, administrators put into place mentorship programs that allow the new teacher to be paired with a veteran teacher. Sometimes the "veteran teacher" may have a few years of teaching experience versus many years. In those situations where a "mentorship" program is in place...new teachers usually will feel more comfortable during that first year because they have a fellow colleague who can answer the many questions they will have throughout the school year.

I hope for you that this will be the situation you walk into on the first day you enter the school. I have been a mentor and I enjoyed being available to the new teachers...mainly because there always seemed to be a question about policy...a question about how to organize the classroom and manage the students...a question that would lead to an answer which hopefully relieved the stress he/she was feeling.

In cases where there are no mentorship programs...then you must be assertive. There are always teachers who are welcoming and who will usually offer themselves to you as a person you can approach and ask questions. I always became defensive if I heard that someone was criticizing the schools by saying that teachers are not friendly. This is such an untruth!

Rather...I would prefer to say that teachers are very busy...pure and simple. Whenever new teachers are hired...the other teachers are still very busy. Some days...open arms are ready for the first year teacher who needs that shoulder to lean on...other days may bring a "not right now" kind of response. Please do not take that to mean that the teacher you are approaching is not friendly or does not want to help you. You can always approach again whenever it is more convenient for the person from whom you are requesting information.

Now...my word of caution to all of you who have just graduated from college after completing your undergraduate degree in education...

Remember...there is much to be learned while teaching and no one ever, ever knows everything when it comes to solutions to problems and advice.

I always felt flattered when the newer teachers would come and ask me various questions...however, I usually was very honest whenever I did not know the answers and when I did not want to offer an answer.

"Did not want to offer an answer...What does that mean???" Well...sometimes, those who have taught for many years will have an answer to your question...but it is not the professional answer or the answer that would be the acceptable one by the principal and administrators. In other words, the only time a veteran teacher should offer advice is when that advice is practical and can be easily applied by you, the new teacher. Opinions can sometimes lead to poor decisions and choices...therefore, be prepared to hear opinions regarding something you wanted to know about and walk away remembering the opinion...but not necessarily following what someone "thought" you should do.

You will understand what I mean whenever you are in that situation. There are days when I felt a little negative about education (there...I have said it). On those days, I may not have been the right teacher to approach and ask, "I have a parent who is being very rude to me on the telephone and has me upset each time I call about the student. What should I do?" Eventually, I would provide the best advice...but I would hope that the new teacher asking me that question would ignore any remark that was not good, professional advice.

I told you whenever you started reading this book...I would always be honest while presenting the chapters. There is one other situation I need to mention...since we are on the topic of honesty...

Remember...you are starting out as a brand new...first year in the classroom...never had students before...teacher.

That means there is a great deal for you to learn. You must also be professional when communicating with your colleagues. Sometimes...new teachers will seek out other new teachers and when gathered together...will criticize veteran teachers. It happens...and you must realize that if you are in a situation that presents this type of "conversation", it would be better for you to walk away.

I have also marveled at how there are a "few" newly hired people who come into a school...first year...and begin to tell...no, I'll use the correct word...begin to dictate what should be done...what needs to change...why something is not working with children. Instead of offering "an opinion"...this type of new teacher appears very aggressive and sometimes presents an attitude that suggests, "I know...I am an authority on the topic."

Think about how you can participate in the discussions that may occur when you attend a faculty meeting or when you work with other colleagues on professional development days. Your energy...your excitement...your knowledge base, especially about computer technology and/or new educational programs and strategies you learned about in undergraduate studies...those things are welcomed by the teachers who want to learn new ideas and are open to your "fresh, new attitude".

I never stopped learning...I am still learning while I teach at Saint Vincent College. The students continue to enrich my thinking...not to mention stimulate thoughts that challenge the way things are being done in the school systems. I welcome the opinions and the questions always...whenever they are offered in a tone that suggests that there is a desire to learn about new ideas.

Yes...there will be days whenever you may want to be by yourself and other days when you may need that helpful other colleague who can assist you in staying in the positive lane. Teachers are a great group of people when it comes to giving a feeling of emotional support and providing a united front regarding the best things that can be done for students.

Be sure to take advantage of those teachers. They are

waiting, just as I did, for the new teachers to relieve them of duty some day. You are our future as well…we are your natural resources you need to tap!

"Talk with other colleagues…accept professional advice and ideas…and remember you are striving to learn about how you can meet the needs of students and parents better each school year."

CHAPTER 9
Merry Christmas, Happy Holiday, Have a Great December!

As you read the title for this chapter, you may be wondering,"What in the world is she going to talk about in this particular part of the book?" Let us say...it is a topic that is very important because it pertains to policies within a school district/private school as they relate to various times of the school year and, in some instances, morals and values.

What interesting times we are leading with regards to progress in education. Whenever I think back to the first few years of teaching, that being in the late 70's and early 80's...I cannot believe how much things have changed. I will also state "education is better than it has ever been...students are learning more, experiencing more, and, in many cases, enjoying learning."

So many times we allow the "nay-sayers" to suggest

that the statement I just made is very false. On the contrary...if we are all honest with ourselves and if we look at how we taught and how students learned 30 to 40 years ago...we have to arrive at that truth that education has improved. The problem, as I see it, is that people tend to want to elaborate on the "wrongs" rather than the "rights". This is a fact in society whenever it comes to most things. One can validate that fact just by turning on the television and/or reading various articles in the daily newspaper. We always seem to be more interested in the negative occurrences rather than the positive ones. We have heard...it is human nature.

In education, the progress that has been made must also be compared to the challenges that have arisen as the improvements occurred. And that leads me to the topic of this chapter...

Whenever you enter a specific school district or private school setting...make sure you learn about policies as they relate to topics such as Christmas and holidays, school prayer/meditation/moment of silence, and certain parts of history as well as pieces of literature that may not be discussed in a classroom. The list I have just noted does not entirely include all the policies that have been changed throughout time due to government laws and equal rights amendments. I have selected these three areas because they are usually the most common ones...the topics that tend to be discussed on television, on the radio, and/or in published articles about schools.

You may be a person who has strong beliefs when it comes to your religion and social practices. However, I would be very wrong telling you that you can state those ideas in front of your students and never experience any repercussions that may be linked with your statements...your teachings. So many times...new teachers did not realize that there was a written policy regarding whether one could say Merry Christmas or whether one could have a moment of silence after the flag salute. In those situations when the new teachers did not know...and they had done something similar to these two examples...objections were voiced by the parents of students who did not have the same "belief systems".

The new teacher then becomes upset and finds it difficult to live by the public/private school's policy that actually opposes his/her own personal belief system. He/She discovers that it is difficult to support the parent's request and, in some extreme cases, is faced with a decision regarding employment.

The best thing you can do...if you are a person who is truly concerned about the practices within a district as they relate to religious beliefs, individual's rights, and personal values...research the district and ask questions during or after the interview. I do believe that those pursuing careers in teaching should research districts that best match their personalities...their beliefs...and their value systems.

Let me make it very clear...this advice is related to your

wanting to know what you may do or not do as it relates to public/private school policy. I am not saying that I, Donna Hupe, do not support Christian morality and values that should be modeled in front of our students. Rather...I am insuring that you understand the significance of knowing what is permitted and what may not be permitted. You are able to make the personal choice of whether you wish to teach in a particular environment or not based on your own belief system.

In most cases, you will find that things are changing in policies and that more discussion is occurring to making positive changes in schools that will motivate students to become wonderful citizens who cherish this great nation and who practice Christian values. Be a part of those changes and work towards bringing about more progress in our educational system as it relates to that important focus.

"Always be aware of the policies your school follows...it is a matter of educating yourself so that you follow the established rules that are in place".

CHAPTER 10
Volunteering...Saying Yes...Saying No

You have finally accomplished what you wanted to do...you have become a teacher. It is your very first year and you are ecstatic!

The first few weeks go quite well. In fact, you are beginning to follow a routine that works for you as a first year teacher. The other teachers in your school are helpful and you like your principal. The students like you as well. Yes...life is good and you are glad you pursued teaching as your career. It is becoming everything you thought it would be.

Then it happens. You are approached to volunteer...to serve on a newly formed committee...to stay after school and tutor students...to help with an extracurricular activity being offered in the community. It may be during that first year...it may happen the second year. You have heard that whenever you are asked to help out...you should do just that. You should make yourself available before school and/or after school when it comes to needs the school district...the community...the students...may have.

It is wonderful when teachers give of their time and their efforts. Many people believe that every school district pays teachers for that extra time. That is not always the case. Budgets are becoming very restrictive...especially when it comes to extra-curricular activities for students. However, there are many teachers who want to see programs continue and who do wish to help by volunteering. That is quite commendable.

I caution you, though, as a new teacher. As wonderful as volunteering might be...remember that you will need your time and energy for learning many new things related to your teaching experience during the first two to three years. You might be able to add one additional activity that might occur prior to/after school...but to add more than one may bring on a great deal of stress.

This also occurs when new teachers serve on more than one committee within a school district. Even though many times the meetings are scheduled during a school day...that still means you have to plan for a substitute. Committees can also present situations that demand completion of work at home or in school before the next committee meeting occurs.

Whatever the case may be...be sure you have prioritized whenever it comes to the students' needs and your needs as the teacher. The first two or three years of teaching place a great deal of demands on a new teacher. These demands are usually linked with writing lesson plans, planning weekly activities, completing clerical responsibilities, and of course…meeting the needs of the students. The time that is necessary to insure that these obligations are met and that all is completed successfully will usually take up most of your days and weeks.

Of course…if you see the opportunity to do something extra for your school that will provide a great change in routine…that will satisfy another professional or personal need you might have…that will provide you with some enjoyment because you get to work with students in a different way…be sure to take advantage of it. The reason for this chapter is to prevent new teachers from saying yes to *every* opportunity that arises and then discovering, after they say yes, that time needed is just not there.

**"When you volunteer, be sure you know
what the activity will include
when it comes to extra time and extra effort."**

CHAPTER 11
Why Should Your Students Listen to You?

The day has arrived! You planned an incredible lesson that is definitely going to hold every student's attention (well, at least the majority of the students in your class). It took a lot of time and effort…but you know it will be the one they never forget. You just cannot wait to see how interested they are in what you have to say and what they have to do in the lesson.

The time arrives for the lesson. The students are looking at you and seemed to be tuned into your "teaching station". You begin the lesson…and then suddenly, as you look up…you notice that a few seem to be looking around the room…someone is doodling on a page…another is playing with something in the desk. It is the moment all teachers dread…the moment when the students appear they are not listening to them.

I have to say...that one of the biggest challenges that teachers face is keeping students interested in learning. I think about the competition we are up against...computers and video games...television and music CD's...after school activities. In the final five years of my teaching career, I discovered that my students seemed to be leading lives that were filled with "entertainment" that was constant and readily available.

Some may not agree that I should refer to those things as competition. However, I have been honest throughout this book and will not stop now...the things I have mentioned above, related to children's and teenagers' personal enjoyment, play a significant role in their lives. Whenever you stop to think about the various activities they may be engaged in during their "lives after school"...it is no wonder that the ways in which we teach need to be evaluated and changed.

I have told my college students and student teachers...think about those activities and lessons you are presenting and ask yourself, "Would you, as a past student, have listened to the teacher who would have taught the way you taught the lesson that day?". Many times...I thought that an activity I had created would hold my students' attention. Some activities did...and others did not. The time spent on the lessons that produced the "less listened to tasks" would have been better spent in thinking about which activities would engage my students in the learning rather than disengage them.

That is truly the key...you have to get your students to "buy into" what you are teaching. That does not mean, by the way, that teachers cannot lecture...that students cannot work on worksheets...that lessons must be television shows each day. Rather, it is a matter of presenting a variety and making sure that your students have good reasons to listen to you as the teacher.

I have been blessed in observing some remarkable teachers throughout my career. Among those teachers...there were those who could present a lecture and never once have a student divert his/her attention from what was being said. How did they do that? They made the lecture interesting.

I know...what an answer! You need to realize that getting students to listen does not mean you need to create some activity that will bring them laughter and lots of fun. Sometimes a lesson can be "too much fun" and no learning occurs.

A great teacher can take a chapter within a textbook and present the information in such a way that the majority of the students in the classroom will stay "tuned in" until the lesson is over. The tone of the voice and the body language are usually what divides the "very interesting teacher" from the "not so interesting teacher". In other words, it is a matter of showing that *you* are interested in what you are saying.

That's right...there are a few teachers who do not appear as though they are interested in what they are teaching. How, then, could the students be interested? In most cases, your students will mirror you. If you are excited about the topic...chances are great that you can get them enthused. And...if you are bored with the subject you are teaching...then the students will model that same boredom.

Will you be able to get all of your students to tune into you each day? I know you know that answer...of course not. However, the greatest majority will listen to you when you present an attitude that suggests that what you are going to say to them is important and something you believe they will enjoy learning.

This is one of those areas...students paying attention to teachers...that will probably be in the top ten list of "Things That Can Stress Me Out as a Teacher". It was for me. The thing I realized very soon was I needed to always keep evaluating my lessons and changing what needed changed so that my students would benefit and learn the concept I was presenting. It is when I made the efforts to do that...I began to see more students truly want to listen to me.

"Think about the lesson that just didn't seem to appeal to your students. Act interested in what you are presenting so that the students might reflect the same interest."

CHAPTER 12
Friend vs. Leader

You may recall that I had mentioned in an earlier chapter the importance of providing a friendly learning environment rather than being a personal friend to each of your students. In this chapter...I would like to elaborate on that thought just a bit more...

I love students! No matter the age group I was teaching...from the tiny ones in Kindergarten to the "growing like a beanpole" third and fourth graders to the "I want to be like..." middle school students...to my college students who were looking for answers...I always enjoyed what my students brought to me as learning experiences. In fact, they are truly the experts who have motivated the writing of this book for new teachers...they are my resources who have taught me so very much so that I could be the best teacher possible.

The one thing I was always cautious about was the

relationship I shared with my students. You will learn very quickly that creating a rapport with students that is lasting and genuine is probably one of the most important ingredients to your success as teacher. The challenge...to build a relationship that, at all times, exemplifies a "friendly feeling...a trusting nature...a caring advisor" as opposed to a "I want to be your best friend...I want you to be my best friend."

You may be asking, "What is wrong with being friends with your students?" The truth is that you can create awkward situations for yourself and the student if you work towards that type of goal.

Let me give you an example. I have seen teachers who do present a feeling of "we are friends...you, the student, and I, the teacher." In those instances it becomes very difficult to create equality among the students when it comes to your relationship with each one. In many cases...the problem is that the teacher begins to show favoritism to certain students because it is almost impossible to establish the same type of friendship with every student. Once there is a feeling of favoritism on the part of some of the students, the breakdown begins to occur in the communication between you and those students. Before the teacher realizes, there is a segmented group in the classroom who truly has no rapport with the teacher. The friendly environment notion is not in place...and the welcome that the teacher meant for every student does not truly exist.

The other reason I question being friends with students is because I believe that teachers are to be looked at as the "leaders" within the classrooms and the school. It is when there is true leadership...not camaraderie...that teachers can take care of the individual needs of each student. You look at your students in a much different way...you have a certain power that you sometimes will keep...you sometimes will share...and, in cases where you have created the ideal classroom which represents student active participation...will give the power over to the students. That cannot be done successfully if your students and you are "pals". They have to have a sense of knowing that someone is in charge at all times.

Teachers can be in charge and at the same time...can have a wonderful, respectful relationship with their students. I am convinced that students are looking for direction from their teachers and do much better when they are aware of the boundaries and expectations. They are then able to joke with their teachers...they can share personal stories and not be ridiculed...they are able to find a purpose in learning and discover that "wanting to find out and know" are wonderful experiences at school.

There are teachers who are still asking themselves, "Why is that teacher able to get the students quiet?" or "How does that teacher keep the students attentive?" Sometimes when a teacher sees the opposite in his/her classroom...noisy, inattentive students...it may be that students believe "anything goes in Mr. So and So's class" or "she will never be mad at us if we…." The result…a classroom that appears unmanaged and depicts "no control" on the part of the teacher.

Remember…you were hired to be a teacher and you are expected to perform as an adult who is the supervisor of students. You are liable for the students at all times and are entrusted with their education. You are an educated adult who has chosen teaching as a career so that you might work with students and create classroom environments that are conducive to learning.

It takes effort to create a classroom that is "welcoming" to all students. So many times…students are looking for friends…that being a reason why it can be hard to not create that type of relationship with students. In the end…you, being a confidant…a caring person…a leader who will go to any length to defend your students…those images will send the message to your students that you can be trusted and be a positive force in their lives.

"Be a great leader among students…pave the way for them and guide them on the paths that will lead them to becoming great individuals with reachable dreams and goals."

CHAPTER 13
Stress Will Come and Stress Will Go

This chapter is so needed when it comes to being a new teacher...in fact, it is needed for all teachers. I believe that this is one of those topics that the public truly does not want to hear about because there is this belief that everyone endures stress.

I will agree with the part "everyone endures stress". However...the difference lies in the types of stress that are created by the amount of responsibility an individual is given whenever he/she is working on the job. Of course...there are other careers (I think of pilots and air traffic controllers, as two examples) which share the types of stress teachers will face. May there be a book that is honest and which truly offers the realistic help to those individuals.

Whenever you walk into your classroom, you will feel so many emotions. I would like to think the first ones you will feel are "happiness and relief you have a job as a teacher". As you stand at the doorway...looking into the room that has become yours...take a deep breath and smile...you are about to start a journey that will be wonderful!

Then...as you attend your first meetings and as you get your list of students...the feeling begins to change, just a bit. You are now realizing that this is not a dream...rather it is a reality that you will be in charge of children's/ teenagers' lives for many months. You will be the person to whom they look for guidance and learning. You also will be the person who will be looked at by parents as the one who will insure that all will be great in school.

Yes...the feeling can be a little overwhelming. Truthfully, that is very normal. I actually can say that I felt overwhelmed every year of the 31 years I taught. Some years brought on more of that feeling than others. I think it is because I always believed I had to make the difference in every child's life...that I had to live up to the expectations of the parents...and that I had to make sure I did all things right when it came to teaching within my schools.

There is nothing wrong with that thinking...it is when that thinking consumes you. That did happen to me...let me briefly tell you about it. Possibly, the story will help you some school year...

I was the teacher and coordinator of the gifted program for a district. It was an incredible part of my teaching...one I cherish because I had the opportunities to work with some wonderful children (grades 1 – 6). I loved being challenged by them, and at times, welcomed the challenges from their parents who were respectful (I never enjoyed those parents who were critical and disrespectful).

Whenever I began...I had about 40 students. I traveled to various schools to service their academic needs and found that in the first 2 years...everything was manageable. However, I also discovered some real truths about myself.

Each year...I strived to make that program better than the past year. In doing that, I added more projects and activities. I worked to individualize the program for every student, as the law would require me to do as a resource teacher for gifted students. I also began to do things after school.

In other words...I turned what occurred in the first 2 years into a responsibility that demanded multi-tasking in every sense of the word. It did not take too long for me to see that in order to do what I was expecting of myself...there had to be three of me with three times the energy levels.

It was the final year of five years when it happened. I was sitting with my supervisor and we were going over the files of all the students. By the fifth year, I had over 100 students on my caseload. Suddenly, I looked up at her, after discussing one of many files...and began to cry uncontrollably...and I do mean...uncontrollably. It is a memory within my soul I shall never forget. I believe I was actually beginning the start of a mental meltdown.

Luckily for me...I had a caring supervisor who motivated me to go into the regular classroom as a teacher. I agreed. Once I did make that move, and got over feeling like I was a failure...the program was changed and more teachers were hired to handle the number of students. I was glad I had shared the concerns and that the district had improved the program by adding more resource teachers.

This happens to teachers many times. You just never read about it nor do you hear about the experiences teachers have had whenever the stress has built to a high that is very harmful. Many will say, "You bring that on yourselves!" and that has some truth. However, teachers become so dedicated to helping students that they sometimes forget that they are humans. That is the real truth.

The good news...you can endure the stress. The key is to accept that there will be challenges ahead and that each year will bring new ones. There will be school years you may want to forget, for more than one reason. There will also be students and/or parents you may want to forget because they caused you to lose sleep various nights.

In the end...remember that you are human and that you have needs. These needs are like your students'...they include emotional, mental, and physical needs. Whenever you begin to feel that things are out of control...be sure to take a weekend and find a way to leave the "school life" so you can renew that spirit I want you to have.

A weekend...you have to be kidding! I said take a full weekend starting after school on Friday to Sunday evening! If it is possible to do this alone...do it. You do not have to run away to some island...if you are in a very stressful mood...you may not return. Rather, you need to quiet your mind. If you can surround yourself with your favorite music...your favorite things to do...your favorite foods (oh, for goodness sakes...it is just for a weekend...just a few foods)...then do that.

The point is this. You have to stop every once in a while to "re-fuel"...to get the positive back...and in many cases, to find some other path to follow the rest of the school year. In the end...you will be grateful that you recognized the problems...the issues...that may be causing the stress that has you on overload.

You can also count on another teacher...that mentor I have mentioned. All teachers have been through some type of stress, one time or another. The great thing I always found when it came to teachers throughout the world...we have a camaraderie beyond all other co-workers in other careers. Take advantage of that whenever you are in need.

The good news...stress will pass by and positive lies around the corner. I promise...things do change...and you are the one to make sure they change for the best. The choices are yours...pure and simple.

The journey as a teacher is one that is filled with tremendous rewards. They will be given to you when you least expect them. It is the rewards that will help you defeat the negatives that can bring on the stress...it is rewards that will keep that passionate flame lit within you.

"Recognize that stress will happen and that there will be challenges along the way as a teacher. Remember to take care of *you* as part of the package of teaching."

CHAPTER 14
It's About You!

It is hard to believe I am now at the end of the book...writing the final chapter. Many have said...it is the last thing you read that can leave the final impression. Alright...let me write a chapter that will give you a lasting impression...

Whenever I think about the 31 years of my life that involved teaching students...I also think about how fast the time seem to pass by me. I shared about my first day with you in a previous chapter. The days from that first moment in kindergarten to the last moment in second grade include so many wonderful memories. It is the positive thoughts that I made sure I came back to whenever I was feeling frustrated, discouraged, and ready to quit. I suggest very strongly you follow that same path.

There are three things I ask you to do as you start the journey as teacher. These things, if followed, should provide you with the types of experiences I have had…moments which were both rewarding and filled with a happiness that was linked with students who benefited by my teaching them during one school year.

First…be sure to always remember that all students come first. I know I have stated this several times in this book. I have decided I am going to stress this one final time. There will be times when you can drift away from that goal. Challenges will come along that can be linked with parents and home…the community and the impacts of the neighborhood…and with the students themselves. However, it is the job of every teacher to do everything humanly possible to reach each student…no matter what the obstacle. That means taking some risks…calling the "not so supportive" parents in to discuss a major issue…working with others to improve the neighborhood and make it a safe environment…and giving everything you have, when it comes to your skills and your emotions, to those students who do not see any value in themselves.

We, as educators, must rally to do all we can to insure that students feel valued. Will you ever find that you cannot reach every student…yes. We are human beings and even though we have been blessed with talents and skills…there are times when other situations and circumstances cannot be changed. In many of these cases…that I believe are very few…teachers and administrators gave 180% effort. The time arrived when they knew they were unable to change what had been "created" around that student.

The key is to make a pledge that these incidences will be very, very few.

The second thing I ask of you is to take care of yourself. That may seem so trite…but I must tell you that teachers are probably one of the groups of individuals who, for whatever reason, go to school not feeling well. They will ignore signs their bodies may be sending because they are dedicated to the cause of educating "their students" within their classrooms.

Now get ready…there will be those in the community who will say there are "many" teachers who take sick days and are not sick. I found that statement was one that could really launch me when it came to defending my colleagues. I have been honest throughout this book…and I have been in the school system for 31 years. I am sure that the few people who continue to put down teachers are those people who never taught one year in the schools. They, for whatever reason, like to take one incident and use it to be the norm…this being something so many people in this world do with regards to many topics or people.

I have witnessed teachers coming in…very ill…worried about making the lesson plans so specific that the substitute and students will have a wonderful day. There have been teachers who have returned early to school, after being ill because they believe they are the only ones who can teach their students (and, in some cases, that can be very true...depending on the types of students in the classroom).

One of my closest friends told me about the year she had pneumonia. She said that she had been going to school each day feeling very tired. Whenever she got home...the rest could not come too soon. Finally, she had to go to an emergency room. The doctor informed her he was transferring her to the hospital...that his diagnosis was pneumonia. She remembers saying to him, "I can't...we are in the middle of testing." And the doctor responded, "Well...you are going...at least for a week".

After a few weeks...she realized she should have taken a few days to be at home and rest. Testing had been the thing that governed her thoughts. It was important that her students did well and she believed that only she could provide the right environment for assessments.

Be sure to be realistic and think about yourself. New teachers during the first year will almost always find they are sick with colds and other illnesses. You will build your resistance with time. It is important that you get enough sleep and that you make sure you respond to your body's needs.

In other words, stay healthy by giving your body what it needs to promote feeling energized and without illness.

The third and final thing I want you to follow...keep that flame within you lit! I began this book with that thought in chapter one. New teachers are always so excited about their first jobs. You feel an incredible happiness within you whenever you are told you are going to be the teacher within a specific school building. That is when the flame will get stronger...for you see, it was lit whenever you started taking courses in college to become a teacher.

Along the journey, there will be challenges. I believe one of the toughest challenges is enduring the "negative people" and their attitudes towards teaching that can sometimes bring about doubts about what you are doing. These include people in the community who are disrespectful and, for whatever reason, choose to criticize teachers. These are the people who usually do not know all that is being done within schools for students.

The other group can be your colleagues. There are only a very small number in this group. They may come to you and challenge the activities you are planning to provide for your students...or possibly they will tell you that you will never be able to do a certain thing because of the students.

Whatever the group of people who are attempting to douse the flame...stand tall and believe that you can do many wonderful things for students...and that, given the experiences and the number of years, you will make a difference when it comes to educating students.

The passion is within you. We all know that there is a great deal that needs to be done if we are to reach every student in our country. It is that passion that will drive you to find the answers...the solutions to the problems that exist. After time...the passion that is now very small will grow and consume you. Your flame will burn within you...and you will be the teacher who will join the incredible group of teachers who are making the difference and who will do all that is possible to lead students to their future destinies they so wish to reach.

"Love being a teacher! Enjoy the journey!"

Donna Hupe plans to write a second book entitled
No New Teacher Left Behind: Part II

If you have a question you would like her
to answer in this book,
please send it to her email address
hoopdtwo@yahoo.com.